OKLAHOMA

It Wasn't Much

True Tales of Ten Oklahoma Heroes

by Jana Hausburg

illustrations by
Cheryl Delany

Forty-Sixth Star Press
Oklahoma City
2008

FIRST EDITION

Cataloging-in-publication Data
Hausburg, Jana, 1964-
It wasn't much : true tales of ten Oklahoma heroes / by Jana Hausburg ;
illustrations by Cheryl Delany ; [series editor, Larry Johnson]
[128] p. : ill., ports. -- (Oklahoma portraits ; v. 1)
Includes biographical references and index.
Summary: "A collection of short biographies which highlight the incredible, real-life adventures of a few heroic Oklahomans, detailing their courage, innovation, and character"--Provided by publisher.
ISBN-13: 978-0-9817105-2-5 (alk. paper)
ISBN-10: 0-9817105-2-2 (alk. paper)
1. Oklahoma--Biography--Juvenile literature. 2. Oklahoma--History--
20th century--Juvenile literature.
3. Heroism--Juvenile literature. I. Delany, Cheryl, 1965- ill. II. Johnson,
Larry, 1966- ed. III. Title.
F693.H38 2008
976.6--dc22

Oklahoma Portraits Series
edited by Larry Johnson

Cover illustration by Stephen M. Prophater

Conceived, written and printed in the
forty-sixth state of the union

www.fortysixthstarpress.com

Preface

In ancient Greece, heroes were humans who were given special abilities by the gods. With superhuman strength and courage, they achieved great deeds which were to be admired by humans for all eternity. In our time, the word "hero" has lost a lot of its meaning, but there are still people among us who are worthy of our praise and admiration because of their accomplishments.

It Wasn't Much is a collection of short biographies which highlight the incredible, real-life adventures of a few heroic Oklahomans, detailing their courage, innovation, and character. Oklahomans have achieved many great things throughout history from the football field to the battlefield. But the heroes in this book were ordinary people who found the strength within themselves to make sacrifices. They risked their reputations and sometimes their lives to help others and to achieve a greater common good. You may not always agree with the reasons these people acted the way they did, but the example they set by fighting for what they believed in is one to which we can all aspire.

We hope after reading this book that you will see that we all have the potential to be as strong and courageous as the Oklahomans whose stories blaze across the pages of this book.

ACKNOWLEDGEMENTS

The author would like to express her gratitude to Ann-Marie Ericksen, Robert Rivers, Willie Rivers, and Betsy Daugherty for their invaluable assistance in writing this book. Special thanks to Jill Vessels, Aaron Killough, Chris Carroll and the Metropolitan Library System's Material Selection Department for reading the manuscript with a critical eye; to Phil, Sullivan and Brennan Hausburg, for their encouragement, and to Jandy, who made it happen.

The publisher would like to express his gratitude to Virginia Rodrigues, Tom Herskowitz, Teri Missildine, the Archidocese of Oklahoma City, and the Carnegie Hero Fund Commission for their cooperation and assistance in producing this book.

CONTENTS

1

ROSEMARY HOGAN
Angel of Bataan

Rosemary Hogan stared at the bushels of apples, marveling at their rich, red color. Her hand trembled a little as she scooped one up and brought it to her mouth. Taking a bite, her teeth sank through the skin and into the juicy fruit. It was delicious, both tart and sweet at the same time. For more than three years, after her capture and imprisonment by the Japanese in a prisoner of war (POW) camp, she had dreamed of this moment.

Fact File

Rosemary Hogan
Born: May 12, 1912
         Walters, Okla.
Died: June 24, 1964
         San Antonio, Tex.

"This is what freedom tastes like," she thought to herself.

What started out as an exciting adventure for a small-town Oklahoma girl turned into a test of courage, resilience and strength. When Rosemary attended Chattanooga High School in Comanche County, she was drawn to the idea of becoming an Army nurse. She didn't have to go far – the Army's Fort Sill was just a stone's throw away in nearby Lawton. By 1936, she was working at Fort Sill Hospital and was eventually assigned to the Philippine Islands in December of 1941. Not long after she arrived, the Japanese bombed Pearl Harbor, Hawaii. The United States was at war.

Rosemary was in Manila, the capital of the Philippines, when the Japanese invaded the islands. Heavy fighting went on for months but she refused

Peninsula

A piece of land surrounded by water on three sides.

to be evacuated to safety. The intensity of the battle pushed the American and Philippine forces back to Bataan **Peninsula** and Rosemary fled with them. There she worked side by side with other nurses to establish the first field hospital on

War in the Philippines

After the surprise attack at Pearl Harbor, Hawaii on December 7, 1941, the Japanese took aim at American forces in the Philippine Islands. They feared the United States could use the islands as a base to attack Japan. An American defeat would also leave Australia and the U. S. west coast vulnerable to attack.

General Douglas MacArthur was in command of several thousand U. S. and Filipino troops. In order to save as many civilians as he could he decided to leave Manila, the capital city, and defend the rocky peninsula of Bataan and then make his final stand at the island fortress of Corregidor in Manila Bay.

The American and Filipino forces fought valiantly against the Japanese, starvation and disease for several months. Finally, on April 9, 1942, Corregidor surrendered. By fighting so long, the troops gave the American armed forces time to regroup and prepare to fight Japan's mighty war machine.

General MacArthur left Bataan in March so that he could organize the armed forces regrouping in Australia. In a famous speech made over the radio to the Filipino people, he said: "I came out of Bataan and I shall return."

Rosemary Hogan tended wounded soldiers like these in the makeshift hospital inside the Malinta Tunnel.

Courtesy U.S. Army Center of Military History

the peninsula. Upon arrival in the mountainous jungle, they found a warehouse filled with medical supplies and equipment. They unpacked and inventoried the supplies and arranged the equipment into hospital stations.

Although Rosemary wasn't the highest ranking nurse, her inner strength and calm made her a natural leader. The nurses worked 18-hour shifts, napping when they could but rarely sleeping. It was difficult to sleep anyway with wounded men streaming in and explosions all around. Soon they ran out of medical supplies. In April, 1942, the tough soldiers and sailors still hung on to Bataan, so the Japanese began a ruthless bombing campaign. Dive bombers targeted the hospital where the nurses worked, even though it was clearly marked

Army nurses put on a cheerful face while boarding a ship for combat duty.

Courtesy Library of Congress

with a big red cross. All but one small section of the building collapsed. **Shrapnel** tore through Rosemary's leg and made a gash above her eye. As she and the other nurses worked wildly to get to the wounded who might be buried in the rubble, a fellow nurse called out to her.

Shrapnel

Sharp metal fragments of exploded bombs or shells

"Hogan! Hogan, is it bad?"

"Just a nose bleed," Rosemary replied, managing to sound cheerful. "How about you?"

Battered by tanks and artillery, the survivors were helped into foxholes by the nurses. They waited for medical attention until the allied American and Filipino forces could evacuate them from Bataan to the nearby island of Corregidor. This island was a fortress built into solid rock with massive guns to protect it and the cavernous Malinta Tunnel underneath. Rosemary helped set up a large hospital in part of this tunnel.

She still wasn't safe, though. Corregidor fell a month later. Just before the Japanese arrived, Rosemary and the other nurses were ordered to evacuate. She tried to escape, but she was captured and placed in a Japanese POW camp when a plane she and the other nurses were taking to Australia was forced down. Her home for the next 33 months was the Santo Tomas Prison in Manila. Many of the soldiers were starving and sick with malaria and were forced to march through the jungle to POW camps. Thousands of them died in what became known as the Bataan Death March.

Conditions in Santo Tomas were brutal. Letters from home were infrequent and food was scarce. Soon the nurses were eating only a handful of rice cooked in milk. Medical supplies were also difficult to find. But Rosemary and her colleagues managed, thanks to the miraculous arrival of Red Cross packages in 1943. Blood plasma, vitamins, liver extract, and bandages – all helped the women continue to do their duty by caring for the victims of the Bataan Death March and soldiers of all armies – even Japanese. The nurses soon became known as the "Angels of Bataan."

In February of 1945, General Douglas A. MacArthur fulfilled his promise to return to Bataan, opening up Manila Bay and forcing a Japanese surrender. Surviving Americans and Filipinos were liberated from the POW camps. Rosemary

THE SCOOP:
LIFE IN SANTO TOMAS INTERNMENT CAMP

Rosemary didn't talk much about what she went through as a POW, but others have shared their experiences.

In June of 1945, American Red Cross worker Marie Adams made a report to the Surgeon General on conditions inside the Santo Tomas Internment Camp in the Philippines. Adams was held in the camp from May, 1942 to February, 1945. The following is an excerpt of that report:

"Among the minor irritants toward the last was the fact that we had to bow to every Jap we met. That seemed to get on people's nerves more than any other single thing...

During the last few months there was a tension among the internees that is almost indescribable. Irritability is one of the first symptoms of starvation, and certainly that symptom was marked among us. We were all cross, irritable, and edgy; we argued about things that were utterly insignificant. We were ready to claw each other's eyes out -- over nothing at all. We were hungry. We were starved. When I went to bed at night, I felt just on the verge of screaming. I ached to the ends of my fingers and toes, with the most horrible ache I had ever experienced. We were so thoroughly depleted that frequently I would sit on my bed and stare at the sink in the corner of the room, wondering whether it would be worth while to make the effort to get up and go over to it and wash my hands...

Everyone was stooped with fatigue. Many had horrible skin conditions. Tropical ulcers and boils were developing everywhere, and infections were on the increase."

Adams, a trained nurse, estimated that if they had not been liberated most internees would have been dead in a few weeks. Because of her exhausting work caring for others, she felt she would have died within four or five days.

Courtesy National Archives and Records Administration

13

ran into the general as she raced around a corner in the prison corridor, dressed in a knee-length house coat she'd fashioned from leftover materials from the Red Cross packages. She was the first nurse to shake MacArthur's hand.

Rosemary Hogan came home to a hero's welcome in 1945. She was awarded a Purple Heart, a Bronze Star for bravery, and a number of campaign medals. In 1958, she became the first female colonel in the United States Air Force.

No doubt Rosemary would agree with Rita Palmer, another nurse who experienced the same horrors, and also received a Purple Heart. "It didn't mean anything," she said. "They all did things, so much more than we did."

After her liberation, Rosemary spent three days of celebration in Hawaii and then was flown with a group of nurses to the mainland of the United States. When she reached California, she was interviewed for a west coast broadcast and mentioned the one thing she dreamed of most during her long imprisonment: apples. Listeners responded by sending her bushels and bushels of apples.

Perhaps that gesture meant more to her than a chest full of medals.

Exploration

Reading

Meyer, Elizabeth. *Teenage Diary Santo Tomas Internment Camp*. Philippine monographs, 1. Claremont, Calif: Paige Press, 2005.

Norman, Elizabeth M. *We Band of Angels The Untold Story of American Nurses Trapped on Bataan by the Japanese*. New York: Random House, 1999.

Internet Resources

Battle for Bataan!
http://reta.nmsu.edu/bataan/index2.html

Corregidor: a Memorial for the Courage, Sacrifice, and Heroism of Its Defenders.
http://www.corregidorisland.com/

Sascha Weinzheimer. The War. Public Broadcasting Service.
http://www.pbs.org/thewar/detail_5192.htm
Sascha Weinzheimer was a child in Santo Tomas during the Japanese occupation.

Places to Visit

US Army Medical Department Museum
Fort Sam Houston, 2310 Stanley Road, Building 1046, San Antonio, TX 78208

Bataan Memorial Military Museum and Library
1050 Old Pecos Trail, Santa Fe, NM 87501

Learn more at our website: www.fortysixthstarpress.com/extracredit.html

2

STANLEY ROTHER
Heart of a Martyr

The white-washed colonial church was crowded. Father Stanley Rother scanned the colorfully-dressed congregation, their brown eyes watching him in expectation. Gripping the pulpit, he raised his voice so that it would easily reach those sitting in the back pews.

"For I was hungry and you gave me food; I was thirsty and you gave me drink. Insofar as you did this to the least of these my brothers and sisters, you did it to me."

> **Fact File**
> Stanley Rother
> Born: March 27, 1935
> Okarche, Okla.
> Died: July 28, 1981
> Santiago Atitlán, Guatemala

Father Rother knew there were people in the crowd who would not like hearing these words written in the Gospel of Matthew. Lending a helping hand in Santiago Atitlan, Guatemala, had become a dangerous act. The priest had already received a number of death threats. Yet he could not leave his people.

"At the first signs of danger, the shepherd can't run and leave the sheep to fend for themselves," he wrote to a friend. Although he did not wish to die, Father Rother could not bear the thought of abandoning his people when they needed him the most.

How did an Oklahoma farm boy end up in such a challenging situation? Stanley was born on March 27, 1935. He was raised on a farm near Okarche with his brothers Tom and Jim and his sister Marita, and developed a love for country life and working with his hands. In high school, he joined the Future Farmers of America, even serving as president of the Okarche chapter when he was a senior. But a greater destiny called to him. After graduating from high school, Stanley decided he wanted to enter the priesthood. He left for a San Antonio seminary.

Civil War in Guatemala

For most of its history, Guatemala was controlled by wealthy landowners and the powerful American-owned United Fruit Company which operated several plantations. The majority of Guatemalans lived as peasants in extreme poverty.

For a brief time (1944-1954), Guatemala was ruled by a reform-minded government which tried to improve the lives of the peasants. Many schools and hospitals were built in the poorest areas. But when the government tried to let workers join unions and to give land to the poor, the landowners and the United Fruit Company became angry. The United States was also concerned because they feared that Guatemala was becoming a Communist country. With American help, Guatemala's military took control of the government and began to rule with a heavy hand.

Resistance to this oppressive rule grew and in 1961, the country fell into civil war. On one side was the military government and on the other were guerrilla groups made up of former military officers and peasants. The civil war brought death and destruction to the tiny country. Death squads murdered anyone who spoke against the government and the military destroyed whole peasant villages. For their part, guerrillas kidnapped and murdered government officials and wealthy businessmen. Meanwhile, the poor, mostly native Mayans, suffered tremendously.

In 1996, after 35 years of strife, the government made peace with the rebel guerrillas. It was agreed that Guatemala would become a democracy and the guerrillas would lay down their weapons and return to their villages. Over 200,000 people were killed during the war and over one million were left homeless.

It was a difficult time. Stanley struggled with Latin. Eventually, he was dismissed because of failing grades.

seminary

A school for the training of priests and ministers

Returning to Okarche, he refused to give up. He worked harder toward his goal and with the help of a kind older priest, he eventually graduated from Mount St. Mary's Seminary in Emmitsburg, Maryland.

Ordained in 1963, Father Rother served several urban Oklahoma parishes, but something was missing. He felt God had called him to use his hands to help the poor, not perform marriages in a big city. In 1968, he heard about the need for a priest in Guatemala. He leapt at the chance to minister to the poor Mayans there, driving his own car for 2,000 miles over terribly broken roads. It took five days.

By the time he arrived in Santiago Atitlan, the Chevrolet's muffler had been completely torn off and the car was in bad shape. Father Rother wasn't worried about the car. Instead, he was overwhelmed by the beautiful surroundings: the gorgeous blue of Lake Atitlan; the spectacular volcanoes; tiny towns nestled on the edges of the lake;

the golden glow of Cerro d'Oro; the friendly faces of the Tzutuhil people. The shepherd had come to the sheep. He was home.

For many years, Father Rother busied himself with serving the people of the village. He worked side-by-side with them, teaching them better farming techniques. He helped establish a medical clinic, started a nutritional center, renovated the church, studied Spanish, and became proficient in the Tzutuhil dialect, even began the process of translating the New Testament into that difficult language. The people began to call him Padre A'plas in their own words.

In 1980, the long-running civil war in Guatemala came to the peaceful mountain village. The small Central American country was ruled by an oppressive military government and a group of rebel generals had begun a war against this regime. None of that mattered to the poor Mayans living in Atitlan; they were just trying to survive. Because he taught these people that they deserved

regime

a mode or form of government

Padre A'plas ministers to children at the mission in Santiago Atitlan

Courtesy Archdiocese of Oklahoma City

a better life, both spiritually and physically, Father Rother learned he was on a death list. Later he witnessed a kidnapping, after which he became marked as a target.

At first, he returned to Okarche, hoping that the danger would pass. He visited his family and his oldest friends. They didn't know it at the time, but he was saying his goodbyes. After a few weeks he told his bishop, "My people need me," and returned to the village.

On July 28, 1981, three masked men slipped into the parish rectory. But it was no secret who they were. Unlike the native Indians, these men were tall and slender. Carrying guns, they forced one of the parish associates to

THE SCOOP:
HOW A SAINT BECOMES A SAINT

Saints aren't born -- they're made.

Some people who live in ways that seem touched by God are given special status by the Roman Catholic Church. The process, called canonization, is very lengthy, and at times has taken decades or even centuries to complete.

The life of a potential saint is investigated for evidence of extraordinary virtue, evaluated by a panel of church officials, and then proclaimed "venerable" (worthy of respect) by the pope.

The next step, called beatification, establishes the facts behind a miracle attributed to the would-be saint. But those martyred (or killed) for their religious beliefs can be beatified without evidence of a miracle.

On top of all that, it takes one more miracle -- but this one must take place *after* the person has died.

Becoming a saint is hard work!

lead them to Father Rother. Terrified, he called out to the priest, "Father, they are looking for you!"

Realizing he was about to be kidnapped, Father Rother made a decision. He would not be taken away to be tortured, killed, and dumped in a field or along the road-side.

23

"Kill me here!" he shouted, opening the door to his bedroom. The three intruders rushed inside. When his kidnappers realized the priest couldn't be taken alive, two shots fired into the night. Father Rother was dead.

On the morning of the murder, 1,000 people gathered in a circle around the church and stood in complete silence. Later, tens of thousands came to say goodbye at Father Rother's funeral. Father Rother's parents wanted their son to be buried in the family plot in Okarche, but the Tzutuhil asked that his heart be buried under the church. That was their tradition. The Rother family understood how important their son had become to the small village of Atitlan and they agreed – his body would lie in Okarche, but his heart would remain in Guatemala. He would always be with them.

The heart of Padre A'plas lies under a marble stone, near the pulpit where his messages of hope once were given. Father Stanley Rother may soon be considered a marytr by the Catholic Church and could one day become Oklahoma's first saint.

Exploration

Reading

Menchu, Rigoberta. *I, Rigoberta Menchu: an Indian Woman in Guatemala.* London: Verso, 1984.

Nouwen, Henri. *Love in a Fearful Land: a Guatemalan story.* Maryknoll, N.Y.: Orbis Books, 2006.

Rother, Stanley. *The Shepherd Cannot Run: Letters of Stanley Rother, Missionary and Martyr.* Oklahoma City, Okla.: Archdiocese of Oklahoma City, 1984.

Internet Resources

United States Department of State. *Background Note: Guatemala.* http://www.state.gov/r/pa/ei/bgn/2045.htm

Pueblo a Pueblo. http://www.puebloapueblo.org/
Pueblo a Pueblo is a non-profit organization dedicated to working with the T'ztujil Maya of Santiago Atitlán, Guatemala.

Archdiocese of Oklahoma City
http://www.catharchdioceseokc.org/

Places to Visit

Holy Trinity Catholic Church
211 W. Missouri, Okarche, Okla.
Father Rother's home parish. A statue has been erected there in his honor.

Learn more at our website: www.fortysixthstarpress.com/extracredit.html

3

FERN HOLLAND
Fearless Warrior

Fern Holland paused in the middle of typing an e-mail message to a friend. She stared out the window of the Babylon Hotel, in Hilla, Iraq, only about an hour's drive south of Baghdad. It was a hot March night, but she had a view of the Euphrates River. Watching the water made her feel a little cooler, but it didn't solve her problem. She needed to find a bulldozer.

With a bulldozer, she could help two widows who had been harassed by a Saddam Hussein loyalist. Their land had been stolen by a man who'd then built a house illegally on the property. Although the widows had a court order, no one would dare approach the man. Fear still hung in the air, despite the liberation of the Iraqi people and the removal of Saddam on April 9, 2003.

Fern turned back to her computer and continued typing:

"So much for the rule of law. I'm going to see him Saturday morning, along with the little ladies, the manager

Fern worked to help women like these who received training and materials for learning to sew in northern Iraq

Photo: Debbi Morello/USAID

of the new women's center, the judge, and a couple of Iraqi policemen."

And, with luck, a bulldozer.

She was only one person, but she was determined to make a difference. Fern was guided by a deeply-held belief that all people are entitled to the same human rights, regardless of where they lived. By participating in simple acts of human kindness and understanding, she believed it was possible to make the world a better place. To her, these were not empty words. Her entire life was dedicated to spreading justice in some of the world's most oppressive places.

Born with Cherokee heritage in Bluejacket, a tiny northeastern Oklahoma farming town, and raised in Miami, where she went to high school, Fern was different from the very beginning. She was the youngest of five children, but she played a big role in supporting her mother during her family's difficult times.

A traumatic divorce split up the family, and may have been the driving force behind Fern's incredible need to be a success. She became an outstanding athlete, homecoming

The Peace Corps

During the Cold War (1945-1990), some people worried that the actions of some American companies and the American government had given the United States a bad reputation around the world. They felt this made it difficult to fight the Soviet Union in the Cold War.

President John F. Kennedy was one who thought that way. During his inauguration speech in 1961, he told Americans, "Ask not what your country can do for you. Ask what you can do for your country." One of his first acts as president was the creation of the Peace Corps. The Peace Corps is part of the U. S. government, but is independent from any other department. Its mission is "to promote world peace and friendship" by sending "men and women of the United States qualified for service abroad" to help poor countries.

Since 1961, nearly 200,000 volunteers (mostly young college graduates) have gone to 139 countries to help achieve the Peace Corps' three goals:
1. Helping the people of interested countries in meeting their need for trained men and women.
2. Helping promote a better understanding of Americans on the part of the peoples served.
3. Helping promote a better understanding of other peoples on the part of Americans.

Peace Corps volunteers build and operate schools and hospitals; teach business, farming, and computer skills; and help restore the environment in their host countries. The Peace Corps provides many Americans a chance to serve their country who are unable or unwilling to join the armed forces.

queen, and salutatorian of her graduating class. She made straight A's and majored in psychology at the University of Oklahoma.

Salutatorian

Student having the second highest rank in a graduating class

Fern was a bold young woman: one who skiied down some of the most difficult slopes, parachuted out of planes 10,000 feet in the air, swam with great white sharks, and jogged alone. Her friends called her "Fearless Fern."

She graduated with honors from the University of Tulsa College of Law, and went on to join a prestigious law firm. In between her schooling, Fern traveled across Europe, worked on an archaeological dig in Israel, volunteered at a children's orphanage in Russia and at a preschool in South Africa.

Fern decided she wanted to work in the area of international human rights. With her law degree and legal skills, she felt she would be more useful in the Peace Corps. In May of 2000, Fern was sent to Namibia in southern Africa. It was there that she experienced the solidarity that came with living among the people. Despite primitive structures, lack of running water and no sewers, Fern felt at home. She often walked more than 5 miles to the closest road, then thumbed a ride to reach the school where she taught, introducing students to traditional subjects and the basic tenets of democracy.

The terrorist attacks of September 11, 2001, changed everything. Within a week, Fern had returned to Tulsa. She and a friend traveled to Ground Zero in New York City. Watching the smoke that rose from the still-smoldering ruins of the World Trade Center, Fern made a decision to go Washington, D.C. She wanted to pursue a degree in international law.

Still, other things called to her. Fern flew to Guinea in West Africa, to help investigate human rights violations. She started a legal clinic there, and helped the American Refugee Committee (ARC) document sexual exploitation of women in refugee camps. It was successful, groundbreaking work, and the ARC wanted her to create more legal aid clinics across West Africa.

The American-led coalition to unseat Saddam Hussein's regime changed Fern's direction. She was recruited by the Coalition Provisional Authority in Iraq as a human rights

The Scoop:
Killing in the Name of Honor

In many countries, the laws of the land forbid women from participating in certain aspects of society; this can range from holding a political office to even driving a car.

The law in some countries even allows a woman's male family members to kill her if they feel she has dishonored them in any way. In Saddam Hussein's Iraq, Decree No. 111 allowed honor crimes by saying, "No person shall be liable to penal prosecution if he kills or commits the premeditated killing of his mother, daughter, sister, and niece to wash out dishonor."

Souad, a Pakistani woman, experienced an honor crime firsthand. She wrote about the horror of being doused with gasoline and set on fire by her own brother. The terror of that day still haunts her.

"I smell the gasoline and I run, the hem of my long dress getting in the way. My terror leads me instinctively away from the courtyard. I run toward the garden as the only way out. I know I'm running and I'm on fire and I'm screaming. But I remember almost nothing after that."

To find out more about her story, read *Burned Alive: a Victim of the Law of Men*, by Souad.

advisor. Her focus would be on serving democracy and the people of Iraq by educating them about how democracy works. Part of her responsibility was to set up women's centers in south central Iraq. The largest and most successful of the centers opened in Karbala in February of 2004.

Fern encountered fierce opposition by Iraqi extremists who disapproved of women obtaining new rights, freedoms, and responsibilities. Some Muslim clerics began to spread vicious rumors about the women's centers; angry men wrote anti-American graffiti on the walls; those helping Fern in her quest were burned in **effigy**; others received death threats.

Effigy

A crude figure or dummy representing a hated person

Her worried friends and family often talked to Fern about her dangerous situation, but she did not want to isolate herself from the people she was trying to help. She refused to live in fortified compounds or travel with weapons and bodyguards.

"I love the work and if I die, know that I'm doing precisely what I want to be doing," she wrote to a friend. She was not deterred in her belief that with faith and tenacity, she would be able to overcome the cultural obstacles in her way to instilling the ideals of freedom in all Iraqis.

On March 9, 2004, Fern found a bulldozer and someone who could operate it. Accompanied by a judge and 30 policemen, Fern watched as the illegal house was demolished.

The constitution of Iraq, seen here, was ratified in October, 2005. Fern helped to draft many of the sections relating to the rights of women.

The widows got back their property and, with time, perhaps the Iraqis would come to trust in the rule of law.

That same afternoon, after visiting the Karbala women's center, Fern drove toward Hilla. With her were Salman Majeed, her translator, and Bob Zangas, a fellow Coalition Provisional Authority employee. On the way, their vehicle was overtaken by a truck and sprayed by the bullets of an AK-47 automatic rifle. Fern and her passengers were killed in what appeared to be a politically motivated assassination.

At her memorial service in Tulsa, the Cherokee Nation of Oklahoma issued a resolution declaring that she had died a "warrior," and honored her "courageous commitment to human rights, and for having sacrificed her life in the service of others."

Fern's work will continue. Her family and friends established the Fern L. Holland Charitable Foundation, which works to provide funds and other support to those causes for which the fearless Oklahoman gave her life.

Exploration

Reading

Al-Windawi, Thura. *Thura's diary: my life in wartime Iraq*. New York: Viking, 2004.

Rubin, Elizabeth. "Fern Holland's War." *New York Times Magazine* 154, no. 52977 (September 19, 2004): 66-138.

Wigton, Scott. "The Better Angel." *Oklahoma Today* 55, no. 1 (January 2005): 30-39.

Internet Resources

Iraq: United States Institute for Peace
http://www.usip.org/iraq/index.html
Find descriptions of U. S. government programs like the ones Fern was working on.

The Peace Corps
http://www.peacecorps.gov/
Learn more about the Peace Corps were Fern began her work.

United Nations Assistance Mission for Iraq (UNAMI)
http://www.uniraq.org/

Places to Visit

Bluejacket Cemetery
Bluejacket, Okla.

Learn more at our website: www.fortysixthstarpress.com/extracredit.html

4

PAUL HENRY CARR
Tin Can Sailor

Paul Henry Carr ran his hands over the blue steel of Gun 52, checking for any flaws or corrosion that might have been caused by exposure to saltwater. Paul was the full-time caretaker of this gun, located aft on the U. S. S. *Samuel B. Roberts*. He was responsible for keeping the

Fact File

Paul Henry Carr
Born: February 13, 1924
   Checotah, Okla.
Died: October 25, 1944
   Samar, Philippines

delicate machinery oiled and ready for battle. Any problems might mean the difference between life and death for the men with whom he served. He wanted to make sure the weapon was in top working order in case the *Sammy B.* encountered the Japanese.

"Still at it, Carr?" asked his commanding officer, Lieutenant Commander Robert W. Copeland, who was making his rounds.

Paul gave a quick salute as the older man gave an informal inspection of the deck of the gun.

The U.S.S. Samuel B. Roberts as it appeared just days before the battle off Samar, the Philippines.

"Spotless, as usual," said the commander. "You take care of that gun the way a meticulous housewife keeps her kitchen and kitchen utensils."

The *Roberts* was a lightly armed destroyer escort which was designed to protect the bigger ships in the fleet from enemy submarines and aircraft while they did the heavy

> **Naval terms**
>
> **Fore and aft**: front and back
>
> **Bridge:** the forward part of a ship from which the ship is navigated
>
> **Turret**: a revolving armored structure on a warship that protects guns mounted in it

fighting. The little escort ships only had two small guns, one **fore** and one **aft**, which could damage an enemy ship. Paul was in charge of the aft gun. He and his crew had the reputation of being the best gunnery crew on the ship; so good, said Lt. Cmdr. Copeland, that "another very good gun crew … looked more or less mediocre by comparison."

Back home in Checotah, Oklahoma, Paul had given as much energy to developing his football skills. The only boy in a family with eight sisters, he'd spent a lot of his time outdoors. He'd painted a bulls-eye on the side of a barn and spent hours long-snapping the ball at it, working on his preci-

Return to the Philippines

"I shall return." These famous words were spoken by American General Douglas MacArthur as he retreated from the Japanese attack on the Philippine Islands in the spring of 1942. After the three years of bloody fighting all around the Pacific Ocean, the Allies were finally ready to make good on MacArthur's promise.

In October, 1944, Allied ground forces attacked the beaches of the Philippine island of Leyte. The Japanese became desperate because the loss of the Philippines would be a serious blow, leaving their homeland open to attack. They decided to send a huge naval fleet to attack the Allied landings and hold on to the Philippines. The resulting battle was the largest naval battle in history – the Battle of Leyte Gulf.

The battle took place over four days involving thousands of men and hundreds of ships, including the massive Japanese battleship *Yamato* – the biggest ship ever built. By the end of the battle, the Japanese Navy had suffered a major defeat and would not play a major part in the rest of the war. The difficult fighting on land for the Philippines could now begin.

General Douglas MacArthur (center) wades ashore at Leyte during his return to the Philippines, October 20, 1944.

Photo: National Archives and Records Administration

sion and accuracy.

His dedication paid off – Paul lettered in football and baseball. He was active in the Future Farmers of America (FFA) and graduated from Checotah High School in May of 1942. At first, he worked for Swift & Co., but he wouldn't be a meatpacker for long. In 1943, he enlisted in the Navy as an Apprentice Seaman. After completing boot camp, he was given leave so he could go back to Oklahoma and marry Goldie Lee Jameson. The couple left for San Diego where Paul enrolled in the naval school to become a Gunner's Mate. At the end of the six-week course, he was promoted to Gunner's Mate, Third Class.

The qualities that had served Paul in the past – dedication, precision, attention to detail – had a way of rubbing off on the members of his gun crew. Unlike the big ships, the destroyer escorts did not have the luxury of a central control system; they had some hydraulic power, but moving, aiming, loading, and firing the gun was mostly all done by hand. One navy veteran described life in the gun **turret** as "orchestrated chaos." Inside the turret it was stifling hot, thin smoke filled the air, an oily mist made everything slippery, and the acrid gunpowder burned the men's eyes and throats. Under those conditions, nearly a dozen men worked to fire fifteen 54-pound shells per minute while the ship heaved with the ocean's waves and the enemy fired back. Paul made his crew practice over and over again. This was not football – in this game, mistakes cost lives.

> **Types of ships**
>
> **Battleship**: the largest and most heavily armed warship
>
> **Carrier**: a warship with a flight deck on which aircraft can be launched and landed
>
> **Cruiser**: a large fast warship with medium armor and guns
>
> **Destroyer:** small fast warship used to support larger vessels

In October, 1944, the *Roberts* was assigned to the Navy's Task Force Three (Taffy 3). Taffy 3 was made up of escort **carriers**, escort **destroyers** and a few standard destroyers. They were keeping an eye on the San Bernardino Strait off the Philippine island of Samar (suh'-mar) while larger fleets were north hunting Japanese aircraft carriers and south supporting the invasion landings on the island of Leyte (lay'-tee). It was supposed to be a quiet sector, but in the early morning hours of October 25th, a fleet of Japanese heavy **cruisers** and **battleships** entered the strait and surprised the lightly armed Americans. At first they tried to escape, but soon Vice Admiral Clifton Sprague ordered his ships to turn and fight. The invasion forces depended on them to hold this position and hold it they would – or die trying.

Against overwhelming odds, the tiny *Samuel B. Roberts* attacked the Japanese heavy cruiser *Chikuma*. Paul's crew fired their gun with amazing speed and precision. Word spread throughout the ship of Paul's leadership and calmness under fire and the whole ship soon became inspired by the hero of Gun 52. The Japanese ship was severely damaged and its **bridge** set afire, but the *Sammy B.* was also hit many times and finally Gun 52 lost power. The order went out to abandon the sinking *Sammy B.*, but Paul refused to leave his post. His crew had already fired over 300 times at the Japanese, and they only had a few more shells left. Only when he had fired everything he had could the Oklahoma gunner accept that he had done his best to fulfill his duty. Paul and crew fired six more times, hoisting and ramming the heavy shells into the gun all by their own weakening strength. As they tried to load another shell, tragedy struck – without power to cool the barrel, it had become so hot the shell exploded inside the gun. Nearly everyone was killed instantly. Paul was severely

The Scoop:
Life in a Tin Can

A destroyer escort (DE) was much less glamorous than the destroyers they accompanied. By navy fleet standards, DEs were pipsqueaks. But men like Paul Carr, who went to war on the undersized ships, soon developed an enormous sense of pride.

Measuring a little over 300 feet, the USS *Samuel B. Roberts* displaced about 2,000 tons of seawater. The ship patrolled the outer edge of a fleet formation, training sonar, radar, and the eyes of her crew to the ocean and sky. Forty to fifty men per compartment slept in bunks that were stacked three high. Neither air-conditioning nor venting were available to make the sailors comfortable. Noise from the boilers could be deafening. Metal bulkheads did nothing to mute the sound. Belowdecks, the sound of dice were sometimes heard as gamblers wiled away the hours. And the quality of food was often less than desirable.

Made from 3/8" steel (which earned them the nickname of "Tin Cans"), the little ships bobbed in rough waters like corks. Before he lost his life on Okinawa, killed by machine gun fire, war correspondent Ernie Pyle described what it was like on a DE in the open ocean: "They are rough and tumble little ships. They roll and they plunge. They buck and they twist. They shudder and they fall through space. They are in the air half the time, under water half the time. Their sailors say they should have flight pay and submarine pay both."

To learn more about destroyer escorts, read *The Last Stand of the Tin Can Sailors*, by James D. Hornfischer

wounded, his body torn open from abdomen to thigh from the explosion. When a rescuer came to pull the men to safety, he found Paul trying in vain to load the last shell into the demolished gun. He took the shell from Paul and then went to help another man, but when he returned to Paul he found him trying again to load the last shell. Paul was laid on the swaying deck of the sinking ship but before he could be put on a lifeboat, the young man died of his wounds.

Paul Carr, the *Samuel B. Roberts*, and Taffy 3 did turn back the Japanese that day. The Japanese were so shocked by the ferocious aggression of these tiny ships, they turned and retreated – they were sure they had met a much larger and more powerful American force. The official historian of the United States Navy said that never in its history did the Navy "show more gallantry, guts and gumption" than that day off Samar. Paul Carr, the 20 year-old farmboy from Checotah, Oklahoma, became the face of that American fighting spirit. He was awarded the Silver Star medal for his actions.

Paul Henry Carr was not forgotten. In 1985, the navy honored him by naming a new ship the U.S.S. *Carr*, one of the few times a ship has been named for an enlisted sailor.

A survivor from the Roberts *is rescued by another Navy ship*
Photo: U. S. Navy Historical Office

Exploration

Reading

Copeland, Robert W., and Jack O'Neill. *The Spirit of the "Sammy B".* Ocala, Fla: USS Samuel B. Roberts (DE 413) Survivors' Association, 2000.

Doscher, J. Henry. *Little Wolf at Leyte The Story of the Heroic USS Samuel B. Roberts (DE-413) in the Battle of Leyte Gulf During World War II.* Austin, TX: Eakin Press, 1996.

Hornfischer, James D. *The Last Stand of the Tin Can Sailors.* New York: Bantam Books, 2004.

Internet Resources

The Battle Off Samar - Taffy III at Leyte Gulf
http://www.bosamar.com/

Destroyer Escort Sailors Assocation
http://www.desausa.org/
lots of history, photos, and personal accounts

Naval Historical Center
http://www.history.navy.mil/index.html
valuable online resources from the Navy's official site

Places to Visit

Destroyer Escort Historical Museum, USS *Slater* (DE-766)
141 Broadway, Albany, N.Y.

Katy Depot Museum & Information Center
North of Interstate 40 on Paul Carr Drive, Checotah, Okla.

Taffy 3 Monument
750 Harbor Boulevard, San Diego, Calif.

Learn more at our website: www.fortysixthstarpress.com/extracredit.html

5

RUTH BROWN
Formidable Librarian

Ruth Brown's face was calm as she slid across the red leather seat of the drugstore booth. Her gray hair was swept back and held firmly in place with a hairnet. Manicured but unpolished nails gripped her handbag. Sitting across from her were two young teachers, Mary Ellen Street and Clara

Fact File

Ruth Winifred Brown
Born: July 26, 1891
        Hiawatha, Kans.
Died: September 10, 1975
        Collinsville, Okla.

Cooke. The teachers were the only African-Americans in Hull's Drug Store that February afternoon in 1950.

The other customers politely ignored the unusual sight of a white woman, their local librarian for almost thirty years, breaking the traditional rules of a segregated northeastern Oklahoma town. The three women waited patiently at the back of the store. They were determined to wait as long as it took. After about ten minutes, the waiter approached.

Ruth smiled.

"I think we're ready to order now."

"Sorry," the waiter said, "But we've called the owner and he says we can't serve you."

Ruth had anticipated this but was unwilling to back down.

"Why?" she asked in a booming voice. The waiter stepped back, surprised by the strength of her tone. She always spoke in a whisper at the library.

"I didn't ask why. He owns the store," the waiter replied, now somewhat belligerent.

Ruth said nothing. The corners of her mouth pulled down slightly as she gave the man a disdainful look. Then the

Jim Crow and Segregation

Even though the Civil War ended slavery, many laws were passed in the former slave states which tried to keep African-Americans from being equal citizens. These laws were called Jim Crow laws after a character from a minstrel show that performed a song called "Jump Jim Crow."

Jim Crow laws varied by state, but they were unfair in any form. Voting rights were denied to non-whites by requiring literacy tests and poll taxes. Because most non-whites could not read or write, they were not allowed to vote. If you could prove that your grandfather had voted, then you didn't have to take the test – but no black person's grandfather had been allowed to vote either.

These laws also segregated (or separated) the white race from other races in public schools and other public places. This meant separate waiting rooms, bathrooms, train cars and schools. Most privately-owned places, such as restaurants and hotels, segregated as well. Before long several generations had grown up this way and both races began to accept things the way they were.

After World War II, the Civil Rights movement grew stronger as people like Ruth Brown and Miss Cooke and Miss Street tried to change things at great personal risk. Jim Crow laws were eventually declared illegal by the federal Civil Rights Act of 1964 and the Voting Rights Act in 1965.

Drinking at the "colored" water cooler in an Oklahoma City streetcar terminal

Photo: Library of Congress

three women stood up and walked out of the drug store, intending to repeat their actions somewhere else on another day.

For Ruth Brown, that day would never come.

Born in Hiawatha, Kansas, Ruth had moved to Alva, Oklahoma, to attend Northwestern State Normal School. She graduated in 1910 and taught school for a while. She eventually went on to the College of Arts and Sciences at the University of Oklahoma, graduating in 1915 with a bachelor's degree. In 1919, after teaching in Eufala and Nowata, she moved to Bartlesville, where both her parents were, and took a job as the library director of the community's Carnegie Library.

Bartlesville's Carnegie Library. Ruth worked here until the library moved in 1927.

Though engaged to be married at one time, Ruth called it off. Her commitment to library work was marriage enough, she decided, and she put all her energy into developing relationships with the people who came to her library to check out books. She especially enjoyed the children. She purchased children's book series that most librarians of her generation would not buy, books such as the Oliver Optic series and the Little Colonel books. She bought a stereopticon and slides for the children's area, and held story times, contests and games in order to encourage reading among her young patrons.

Sometimes she seemed a little **formidable** to children, insisting they whisper and behave themselves appropriately in the library. But she also had

> **Formidable**
>
> Causing fear, dread, or apprehension; also Tending to inspire awe or wonder

a reputation for being kind. She mentored young people by giving them library jobs and encouraged them to go to college. She made sure she knew everyone's names, and kept in touch with her protégées long after they had gone on to other things. Ruth wasn't afraid to break some of the rules at times.

She once let a youngster with an overdue fine check out a book using a relative's card.

Ruth eventually adopted a young girl, Ellen Holliday, who had been orphaned after the death of her mother. She became a foster mother to Ellen's older sister, Holly Holliday, as well. Her daughters remembered Ruth's endless energy. She constantly seemed to be doing something, whether it was reading, bird-watching, playing Scrabble or other games, or doing needlework. She was sometimes bold, sometimes shy, often blunt, but always committed to offering the library and its contents to her community as a "recreational culture suited to all needs."

Early on, Ruth demonstrated an unusual dedication to providing information to all members of Bartlesville, including African-Americans. With the approval of her library board, she offered segregated story hours for children, traveled to Douglass School to read to the African-American children who attended there, and eventually brought those same children into the library to let them borrow anything they wanted from the library collection. Her commitment may be attributed to a reading of Richard Wright's book, *Black Boy*, pub-

THE SCOOP:
"SEPARATE BUT EQUAL" IN THE LIBRARY

Richard Wright was an African-American author who wrote about his experiences growing up in the south during the early 1900s.

Segregation was strictly enforced by Jim Crow Laws, state and local laws put in place that mandated "separate but equal" status for black Americans. In reality, there was nothing equal about these laws.

When Richard Wright wanted to borrow a book from a Memphis library, Jim Crow Laws of the time did not allow him to have a library card. Instead, he had to borrow a card from a white man in his office and pretend to be checking out books for his co-worker. The librarian was suspicious. Fear coursed through Richard.

"Perhaps she would not let me have the books? If she had turned her back at that moment, I would have ducked out the door and never gone back."

Instead, Richard challenged the librarian to call his co-worker. Satisfied, she stamped the card and handed him the books he wanted. Reading those books by H.L. Mencken changed the direction of Richard's life.

"What was this? I stood up, trying to realize what reality lay behind the meaning of the words...Yes, this man was fighting, fighting with words. He was using words as a weapon, using them as one would use a club. Could words be weapons? Well, yes, for here they were. Then, maybe, perhaps, I could use them as a weapon?"

To learn more about his experiences, read *Black Boy*, by Richard Wright.

lished in 1945. She was struck by a passage in which Wright remembers having to pretend to get books for a white man in order to gain access to the library.

"How can a librarian read it and not be influenced, and how can anyone fail to see that freedom to read must include all who have that desire?" she wrote in a 1961 letter to *Library Journal.*

Ruth helped form the Committee on the Practice of Democracy (COPD) in order to improve "relations among people of all races." The two African-American teachers were members, too. Together they crossed the color line and asked to be served at Hull's Drugstore.

The country was about to undergo a difficult period. Senator Joseph McCarthy was beginning to accuse members of the government as having Communist ties. This reaction to the Cold War created tension all over the country, and it provided opponents of Ruth's activism with an excuse to attack her. The fact that she was a woman, and unmarried, made her actions more suspect in a town where women were traditionally expected to remain out of the public eye.

At a Bartlesville City Commission meeting, a group of citizens charged Ruth Brown with supplying "**subversive**" materials to impressionable young minds

Subversive

An attempt to overthrow a government or political system by persons working secretly from within

at the public library. Magazines such as the *Nation*, the *New Republic*, and *Soviet Russia Today* were offered as evidence. A few days later, a photograph appeared in the local newspaper featuring stacks of the "offensive" magazines, plus two books about Russia that were never located in the library collection. Many years later, it was learned that these books came from the Tulsa Public Library. The library board had never authorized the taking of such a photograph. How the newspaper photographer gained access to the library is still a mystery.

The next few months descended into bitter accusations and angry attacks. The library board did all it could to defuse the situation by moving the controversial material to locked storage, but the citizens' committee was not satisfied. The entire board was dismissed and a new set of members appointed who did not like Ruth Brown's civil rights activism.

At the end of July, Ruth was brought before the city commissioners. She was interviewed about her interracial activities, her loyalty to the country, and her book buying policies. Within an hour, Miss Ruth Brown was out of a job. According to the city mayor, E.S. Dunaway, the librarian had refused to respond to questions about her personal life unless they were put in writing. Dunaway said he found Brown's answers verged on "insubordination."

Although she sued the city in a lawsuit that went all the way to the Oklahoma Supreme Court, Ruth failed to re-

African-Americans were finally allowed to use the Bartlesville Public Library several years after Ruth Brown was fired.

gain her job. It appears she knew that by pushing integration, she would risk serious consequences. As she told a friend, "It might mean that I would no longer be Bartlesville's librarian, but I've had that fun for thirty years anyway."

Ruth's story caught the eye of Hollywood, resulting in the production of *Storm Center*. The film featured Bette Davis as she battled pressure to remove subversive and communist materials from her library. The issue of racial equality was considered too controversial to include.

After Bartlesville, Ruth continued her career as a librarian, first at an African-American school in Jackson, Mississippi, and later as a public librarian in Sterling, Colorado. She retired at the age of 70 and eventually moved to Collinsville, Oklahoma to live with her daughter, Ellen. She died there at the age of 84, and donated her body to the University of Oklahoma Medical Center.

Every year, the Oklahoma Library Association honors Ruth Brown's courageous efforts to integrate public library service in the town of Bartlesville, Oklahoma, by giving an award in her name. The award recognizes programs that address issues of social concern.

Exploration

Reading

McClaurin, Irma, and Virginia Schomp. *The Civil Rights Movement*. Tarrytown, N.Y.: Marshall Cavendish Benchmark, 2008.

Robbins, Louise S. *The Dismissal of Miss Ruth Brown: Civil Rights, Censorship, and the American Library*. Norman, Okla: University of Oklahoma Press, 2000.

Wiegand, Shirley A., and Wayne A. Wiegand. *Books on Trial: Red Scare in the Heartland*. Norman: University of Oklahoma Press, 2007.

Internet Resources

Oklahoma Library Association Social Responsibilities Roundtable's Ruth W. Brown Award
http://www.oklibs.org/~srrtola/rb.html

Southern Poverty Law Center Civil Rights Memorial
http://www.tolerance.org/memorial/
a multimedia guide to the Civil Rights movement

Turner Classic Movies Database: *Storm Center*
http://www.tcmdb.com/title/title.jsp?stid=91490

Places to Visit

Ruth Brown sculpture
Bartlesville Public Library
600 South Johnstone, Bartlesville, Okla.

Bartlesville Area History Museum
City Center Building, 5th Floor
401 South Johnstone Ave, Bartlesville, Okla.

Learn more at our website: www.fortysixthstarpress.com/extracredit.html

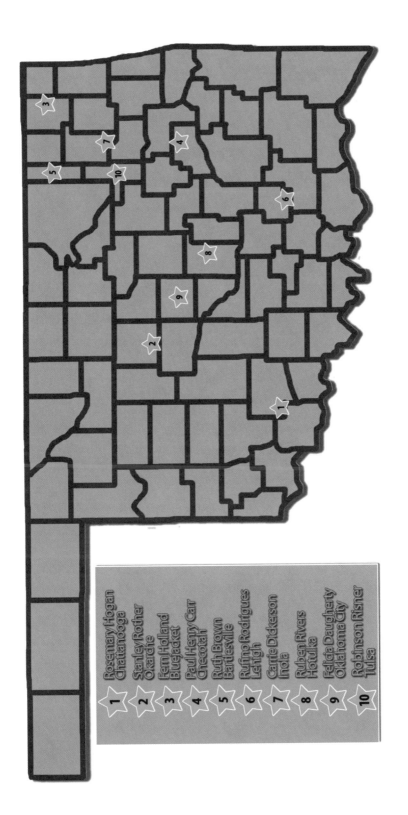

	Rosemary Hogan Chattanooga
1	
2	Stanley Rother Okarche
3	Fern Holland Bluejacket
4	Paul Henry Carr Checotah
5	Ruth Brown Bartlesville
6	Rufino Rodrigues Lehigh
7	Carrie Dickerson Inola
8	Ruben Rivers Hotulka
9	Felicia Daugherty Oklahoma City
10	Robinson Risner Tulsa

6

RUFINO RODRIGUES
Oklahoma Orpheus

On February 22, 1912, an explosion ripped through a mine near the sooty town of Lehigh, Oklahoma. More than 300 feet below, fire swept through the mine's passageways.

No one knew exactly what started the fire in Lehigh's No. 5 mine that morning. According to some sources, a care-

> **Fact File**
> Rufino Rodrigues
> Born: February 29, 1890
>   Mexico
> Died: August 20, 1980
>   Broken Arrow, Okla.

less coal miner ignited a barrel of car grease, which had been set near a steam-operated heater to warm. The fire spilled over and spread across the ground to timbers not far from the bottom of a deep shaft. In a flash the fire had spread to several tons of hay, which had been stored to feed the mules that were stabled underground. The mules were there to pull heavy cars of coal to the surface.

The men who were working nearby knew they were in a very dangerous situation. Several hundred feet below the surface of the earth, in cramped quarters and terrible darkness, a fire in a coal mine could bring about death by **suffocation**. Immediately, the miners began rushing to the metal cage used to hoist them out of the shaft.

Suffocation

To die from being unable to breathe or from lack of oxygen

One man, Rufino Rodrigues, ran the other way. He hurried down a slope in an attempt to sound an alarm. There were nearly 250 men working further inside the mine, many of whom were immigrants from Italy, Russia, Poland, and Mexico. Working downwind from the fire would mean they would have little or no warning of the coming inferno. They would have no time to find an escape. Although the choking fumes from the smoke were enough to knock him over, Rufino refused to desert his fellow workers to a certain death. In his heart, he believed the others would have done the same for him.

Rufino was born in Mexico and came to America when he was only a few months old. His parents were like many poor immigrant families in the early 1900s and had not been able to pay for him to get an education. So, Rufino made a living by working in the coalmines. Because of the difficulties some immigrants had in communicating with Eng-

Photo: National Archives and Records Administration

Miners entered and exited the mine shaft through small elevators like the one seen here.

Child Labor in the Coal Mines

The term "child labor" refers to the use of children under the age of fifteen to work long hours in factories or mines. One reason children were used as workers in the mines was because their small size allowed them to move about more freely in the small spaces underground. Mainly it was because they were easily controlled and would work for very little wages.

Boys as young as eight years old worked 10-12 hours per day in the mines. While few boys this small actually mined coal, they performed various other chores. Some drove mules which pulled cars through the mine's chambers; some shoveled coal into the cars; some worked in teams as "breaker boys." Breaker boys sat in a crouched position as mined material flowed under their feet. They picked the pieces of rock and other junk from the chutes so that only clean coal passed through. Cuts, broken fingers, and much worse were daily hazards. This was all done in near total darkness for about 75 cents per day.

By 1910, activists began to campaign against child labor and before long many Americans viewed child labor practices as a form of slavery. Soon laws were passed which strictly limited the hours and work children could perform. In many parts of the world today, however, children still work under terrible conditions in mines.

Young breaker boys working in a Pennsylvania mine in 1911.

Photo: National Archives and Records Administration

lish speaking bosses and mine owners, many were "entirely ignorant of mining" and had no knowledge of the dangers they would encounter, according to a U.S. Senate report from 1908.

Despite his lack of education, Rufino made an impression on those around him. He seemed to have natural leadership abilities. Edward Boyle, who was a state mine inspector, said of the young man, "You didn't need to have that fellow pointed out to you. You could see him in a crowd, and guess there was something to him."

In Oklahoma, coal mining had a reputation for having one of the highest **fatality** rates of any other major industry operating in the state. Coal dust was a potentially explosive hazard and could be set aflame when dynamite was used to carve out additional tunnels. When there weren't enough wooden roof pillars, cave-ins were common. Gas explosions and fires often broke out in the mines, leaving behind poor widows and fatherless children.

Fatality

Death resulting from a disaster

This time, Rufino hoped there would be no widows and orphans. Remembering a partially collapsed passage that he believed would take him around the fire to the trapped men, he felt his way along a tunnel that was about a mile and a half long, keeping just ahead of the smoke. He filled his dinner bucket with water and carried it with him. From time to time, he would wet down his wool shirt and use it to cover his face.

On the surface, rescue teams decided the fire was so great that theirs would be a recovery mission, not a rescue. They didn't know about Rufino Rodrigues. He refused to give up. When he ran into a partially blocked passage, he began digging through rubble with his bare hands. Finally, he reached the other men and told them of the danger. Some of them did not even know the mine was on fire! Many of the miners spoke only French or Italian and they nodded at his shouts and then turned back to their work. But somehow Rufino found a way to make them understand.

The situation was beginning to get desperate. Smoke was now so dense in the tunnels that Rufino began stumbling over bodies of men who had been unable to escape. Com-

THE SCOOP:
WHAT'S IT LIKE IN A COALMINE?

English author George Orwell, who wrote the classic dystopian novel *1984*, visited a coalmine in the 1930s. He described what went on below ground was "like my own picture of hell … heat, noise, confusion, darkness, foul air, and, above all, unbearably cramped space." Men worked bent over or on their knees due to the low ceilings. Coal dust clogged up nostrils, throats, and eyelids, and a "dusty fiery smell" hung in the air. Walking from one shaft to another meant hunching over while keeping an eye upward to watch for beams, girders, and rocky outcroppings. "You have, therefore, a constant crick in the neck, but this is nothing to the pain in your knees and thighs." Often, the miners banged their backbones on the top of the passageways, developing "buttons down the back," which referred to permanent scar tissue on each vertebra of the spine. The shiny black wall face of the coal ledge stretched on into the darkness as the men worked with picks and shovels to get the coal out of the rock.

From George Orwell's *The Road to Wigan Pier*.

pletely exhausted, he finally made his own way to the last exit down a two-mile long passageway. Hours had passed since the outbreak of the fire. He collapsed at the opening just as the last man got out, but was quickly dragged to safety.

"The last I remembered was when I grasped the ladder. When I grew conscious, I found myself lying under the open sky, and my father was there talking to me. Dead men were lying round me," Rufino said later to a newspaper reporter.

Nine men died that day, but Rufino Rodrigues directly saved over 150 miners. He received many accolades, including a $100 gift from the Lehigh miners and a medal from the Carnegie Hero Fund. For many years, the wives and children of the men he had rescued would come up to him and shake his hand, so grateful for his extraordinary feat. But anytime people asked him about that day, this Oklahoma hero simply grinned and said, "It wasn't much."

Rufino received a bronze medal like this one from the Carnegie Hero Fund

Photo: Carnegie Hero Fund Commission

Exploration

Reading

Bartoletti, Susan Campbell. *Growing Up in Coal Country*. Boston, Ma.: Hougthon Mifflin Co., 1996.

Gunning, I.C. *When Coal was King: Coal Mining Industry in the Choctaw Nation*. Okla.: Eastern Oklahoma Historical Society, 1975.

Kalisch, Philip A. "Ordeal of the Oklahoma Miners: Coal Mining Disasters in the Sooner State, 1886-1945." *The Chronicles of Oklahoma*. 48 (Autumn, 1970).

Internet Resources

The Carnegie Hero Fund
http://www.carnegiehero.org/

Coal Mining in the Gilded Age and Progressive Era
http://ehistory.osu.edu/osu/mmh/gildedage/default.cfm
historical documents describing conditions in coal mines

Old Ben #17, The Museum of Science and Industry
http://msichicago.org/exhibit/coal_mine/descent.html
take a virtual tour deep inside a coal mine

Places to Visit

Coal County Historical & Mining Museum
212 S. Broadway, Coalgate, Okla.

Oklahoma Museum of Mining and Labor
Henryetta, Okla.

Learn more at our website: www.fortysixthstarpress.com/extracredit.html

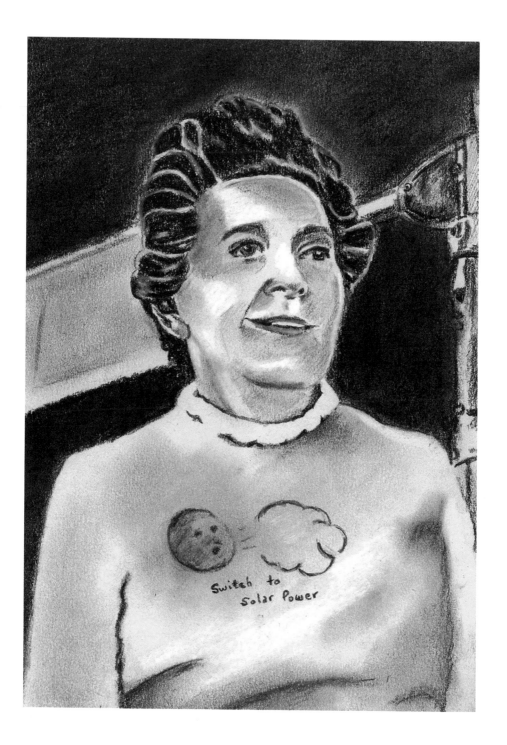

7

CARRIE DICKERSON
Showdown at Black Fox

The repetitious motion of the needle moving through fabric and cotton batting helped calm her nerves as Carrie Barefoot Dickerson focused on making tiny, perfect stitches. That was the way her Grandmother Perry had taught her more than half a century ago. Still, no one

Fact File
Carrie Barefoot Dickerson
Born: May 24, 1917
    Okmulgee, Okla.
Died: November 17, 2006
    Claremore, Okla.

was fooled by the serene bow of her gray head. Her true attention was not on the quilt in her lap but on the men who were testifying in front of the Advisory Committee on **Nuclear** Safeguards (ARCS) hearing. They were determined to plow through the wall of opposition against bringing a nuclear power plant to Oklahoma. Equally determined was Carrie, who was the primary reason for the delays behind the building of the Black Fox nuclear power plant. She had vowed to do everything she could to stop it.

> ## Nuclear terms
> **Fission**: splitting the nucleus of an atom
> **Neutron**: an uncharged particle present in an atom's nucleus
> **Nuclear**: related to or produced by an atomic reaction
> **Nucleus**: the central portion of an atom containing the protons and neutrons

One spring morning in 1973, Carrie was a busy supervisor at Aunt Carrie's Nursing Home in Claremore, Oklahoma. She and her husband, Robert, had built the facility themselves and Carrie had studied to become a registered nurse so she could care for the elderly residents. It was there that Carrie came across a newspaper article declaring in black, bold letters: "$450 million N-plant for Inola." The tiny farming community of Inola was less than thirty minutes east of Tulsa, the second most populous city in Oklahoma. It was just thirteen miles from her home in Claremore,

After reading the article, a long-buried memory surfaced in Carrie's mind. She remembered reading about a muskrat which had developed

Resolve

Determination; having one's mind set on a single purpose.

cancer after receiving a dose of radiation from a Tennessee nuclear facility. "If radiation would give cancer to a muskrat," she thought, "what would it do to me and my family?" The sight of her two-year-old grandson playing outside in the grass only strengthened her **resolve**. She would do whatever she could to keep him and future generations safe.

Carrie was not an activist. But after reading *Silent Spring*, Rachel Carson's groundbreaking book on the terrible effects of pesticides, she developed a habit of cutting out articles on environmental issues and keeping them in a scrapbook. She knew nothing about nuclear power, and threw herself into research. A quick phone call to the Atomic Energy Commission resulted in packets of information being

Nuclear Power Plants

Nuclear power generation is a relatively new technology. The neutron itself was discovered in England in 1932. Soon after, scientists learned that splitting the neutron of an atom created energy. A race began during World War II to build a powerful bomb using this new energy source. Nazi Germany came close, but it was the United States which developed and used the first atomic bomb in 1945.

After the war, many scientists tried to harness nuclear energy to generate electricity. The world's first nuclear-generated electricity lit up four light bulbs at an experimental reactor in Idaho in 1951. In 1954, the world's first nuclear power plant in Obninsk, Soviet Russia, began generating electricity for consumer use. The first full-scale American nuclear power plant was built near Shippingport, Pennsylvania in 1957.

From the 1950s through the 1970s, nuclear energy was seen as the answer to the world's energy needs. It is cheap to produce and does not contribute to air pollution like fossil fuels do. However, environmentalists became concerned about long-term effects such as the storage of radioactive waste which can last for thousands of years. Accidents like those at Three Mile Island in Pennsylvania and Chernobyl in the Soviet Union, also increased fears about safety.

For most of the 1980s and 1990s, nuclear power was in decline, but today there is renewed interest because of the increasing cost and scarcity of fossil fuels and improved nuclear technology safety measures. In 2007, several new American nuclear power plants were given the approval to begin construction.

mailed to her every week. She joined the Oklahoma chapter of the Sierra Club and was recruited into the Friends of the Earth organization. Then she prepared herself to attend the first public hearing on the proposed Black Fox plant.

The more Carrie studied, the more she became convinced of the dangers of nuclear power. She learned about the difficulties involved with safely

Radioactivity

Rays emitted by the disintegration of an atom's nucleus

storing the highly **radioactive** by-products of nuclear power generation. She read that terrorist groups might obtain and use the by-products to contaminate other countries. She also learned of the fact that radioactive waste lasts for thousands of years, poisoning the earth and possibly generation after generation of children.

Carrie became convinced that there was a safer, more viable alternative to nuclear energy: wind power, solar energy, and conservation. As she sat through endless public hearings, Carrie couldn't help thinking there was a better way that they all could be spending their time. How much cheaper, how much easier, how much safer, she mused, if they simply put up windmills instead of spending all this time, effort and money figuring out how to cope with a nuclear disaster.

As the fight progressed, Carrie found herself consumed by anger. When she tried to sleep, she had terrible nightmares. She was bitter that those in power would place ordinary citizens at such risk. Hadn't she always believed that the government would represent her and look after her well-being? In her naiveté, she had never imagined a betrayal of this magnitude.

Even worse was the attitude of those at the Public Service Company of Oklahoma (PSO). When she called PSO President R.O. Newman to talk about her concerns and her plans to stop the construction permit, he was unimpressed.

"Nothing can stand in the way of the completion of the nuclear power plant," he said.

Soon she was so depressed and ill, she could barely carry out her duties at the nursing home. She knew that she had to redirect her anger into something positive. Holding grudges against the officials determined to build the plant would only make her sicker. She remembered her own mother's words of wisdom, taken right from the Bible -- "Love

THE SCOOP:
THE CHERNOBYL DISASTER, 1986

It's considered the worst nuclear power plant accident in history. On April 26, 1986, there was an explosion in the reactor at the Chernobyl Nuclear Power Plant in Ukraine (then the Soviet Union). A plume of radioactive particles shot into the air and drifted over parts of Russia, Europe, and eastern North America. Radioactive contamination threatened those living nearby. Over 336,000 people had to move away.

More than 60% of the radioactive fallout landed in Belarus, a situation the government was not prepared to deal with on such a massive scale. As a result, tens of thousands of ordinary citizens were exposed to massive doses of radiation.

Citizens who were evacuated and later returned reported strange phenomena such as die-offs of all the sparrows, black rain clouds that left behind puddles of yellow and green, and radioactive leaves.

When interviewed, one eyewitness talked about the strange glow seen the night of the reactor melt-down.

"This wasn't any ordinary fire, it was some sort of shining. It was pretty...we didn't know that death could be so beautiful."

To learn more, read *Voices from Chernobyl: the Oral History of a Nuclear Disaster,* by Svetlana Alexievich.

thy neighbor as thyself" -- and Carrie prayed for a change of attitude.

Finally able to channel her anger more positively, Carrie began to view the PSO people as neighbors. "I was fighting an issue, not people," Carrie said. She called on her faith to give her tranquility and inner peace. Some people could not understand how she could fight so hard against PSO during a hearing, then sit down and laugh with the company's president during a recess. "Why are you treating him like a friend? Don't you realize he's the enemy?"

Three Mile Island Nuclear Generating Station, site of the worst nuclear accident in United States history in 1979

Photo: U.S. Department of Energy

She refused to believe that way. As Carrie saw it, nuclear power was the enemy.

Others came to believe that she was right. Carrie founded a group called the Citizens' Action for Safe Energy (CASE) and gathered many like-minded allies to join the fight. They held demonstrations and organized non-violent protests. They drafted petitions and gathered signatures at rallies, fairs, and even the supermarket. Carrie met with congressmen, senators, and other Oklahoma legislators, tirelessly educating them about the dangers of nuclear power and the benefits of safe, renewable energy sources.

Fighting such a well-funded industry was expensive. Carrie backed up her actions with her own finances, eventually selling the nursing home to raise money for the legal challenge. She sent out fundraising letters, raffled off quilts she made by hand, and eventually mortgaged the family farm. In the end, she spent over $550,000 of her own money.

In the middle of her struggle, Carrie's beloved husband of 43 years died of a stroke. She refused to allow herself time to mourn, though. She walled up her grief until she was victorious in the fight against Black Fox.

Delay after delay began to cost the PSO dearly, and eventually the company made a request to the Oklahoma Corporation Commission (OCC), which regulates utilities in the state. The company asked for a utility rate increase to help finance the power plant's construction. After a lengthy hearing, in which Carrie and many others testified, the OCC declared that the Black Fox nuclear power plant was no longer worth the expense. After a nine-year battle, Aunt Carrie had won!

A dedicated peacemaker, known for treating people with dignity and respect, Carrie Barefoot Dickerson remained active in educating the public about safe, renewable energy until her death at the age of 89.

Carrie was a supporter of clean and renewable energy sources like this wind farm.

Photo: Washington Department of Fish and Wildlife

Exploration

Reading

Dickerson, Carrie Barefoot, and Patricia Lemon. *Aunt Carrie's War against Black Fox Nuclear Power Plant*. Tulsa, Okla: Council Oak Pub, 1995.

Dickerson, Carrie Barefoot, Patricia Dickerson Lemon, and Gwen Ingram. *Harvesting the Wind: Fourteen Centuries of Wind Power*. Warwick, Mass: Patricia Dickerson Lemon, 2006.

Internet Resources

Anti-Nuclear Energy Sites

Greenpeace International: End the Nuclear Age
http://www.greenpeace.org/~nuclear

National Resources Defense Council
http://www.nrdc.org/nuclear/default.asp

Pro-Nuclear Energy Sites

American Nuclear Society
http://www.ans.org/

Nuclear Energy Institute
http://www.nei.org/

Places to Visit

American Museum of Science and Energy
300 S. Tulane Avenue, Oak Ridge, Tenn.

National Atomic Museum (National Museum of Nuclear Science & History)
1905 Mountain Road NW, Albuquerque, N. M.

Learn more at our website: www.fortysixthstarpress.com/extracredit.html

8

RUBEN RIVERS
Courage and Valor

It was dawn on November 8, 1944: northeastern France. A group of tanks came upon a roadblock. A large tree had been dragged across the road and was laced underneath with landmines. It was partially cloaked by dust kicked up by blasts of artillery and smoke from mortar fire.

Fact File
Ruben Rivers
Born: October 30, 1918
Tecumseh, Okla.
Died: November 19, 1944
Guebling, France

Due to heavy forests on either side of the road, maneuvering around was impossible. Ruben Rivers, Staff Sergeant in the 761st Tank **Battalion**, an African-American tank battalion, watched as Germans behind the blockade cut down American infantrymen stranded in open ditches along the road.

> **Armored Units**
>
> **Platoon**: a unit of four tanks
> **Company**: a unit of three tank platoons
> **Battalion**: a unit of three tank companies and a headquarters
> **Division**: a large unit made up several smaller units

And still the tanks could not move.

Ruben was sick and tired of waiting. Sick and tired of having to prove that he was ready to fight. Sick and tired of waiting for the Army to see that his **company** of African-American soldiers was fit and able to serve on an equal footing with their white counterparts. Sick and tired of the overt racism expressed by his general, George S. Patton, who had written, "A colored soldier cannot think fast enough to fight in armor."

They were headed for Vic-sur-Seille, and had been chosen to join with the 104th Infantry **Division** by General Patton. They would take part in his Saar Campaign in an ef-

The Saar Campaign

After the successful D-Day landings in June, 1944, the Allies got a foothold in Europe and the German army fell into a confused retreat. Throughout the summer, the Germans were on the run with the Allies not far behind them. By the fall of 1944, the Allied war plan was to keep pushing the retreating Germans along a wide front stretching from Holland to Switzerland.

As part of that plan, General Patton's Third Army began the Saar Campaign. It was fought in the northeastern section of France in the Saar River valley near the border with Germany. Conditions for battle were terrible. One serious problem was the lack of supplies and fuel. The Allies had been moving so fast, their supply line could not keep up. Another was the lack of replacement soldiers after the heavy losses at D-Day. The problem no one seemed to be able to do anything about was the weather. Cold, rain, and snow hampered the soldiers and many Frenchmen said it was the worst weather they had ever seen.

The campaign was one of fiercest of the war. Tanks have trouble fighting in forests, and the roads in the area were clogged with mud or washed out by floodwaters. The many streams in the area were swollen and the retreating Germans blew up most of the bridges. This made it easy for the Germans to block roads and trap the tanks. As difficult as it was, the superior leadership of General Patton and the strong fighting spirit of men like those in the Black Panthers led the Allies to victory in this campaign.

A Sherman tank navigates a muddy road during the Saar Campaign, November, 1944.

Photo: U. S. Army Center for Military History

fort by the Allies to drive to the Siegfried Line. The only route forward was now blocked, keeping the 104th from advancing. In this kind of situation, the Army's rules were clear: the infantry was responsible for making the surrounding area safe enough to remove the roadblock; the tanks were to hang back and shoot shells to cover the infantry. Ruben knew it could take several hours to do things the right way. He also knew it would mean more waiting and more dying.

Flinging back the hatch on top of his tank, Ruben hopped out, dropped to the ground and took hold of his tank's tow cable. Calm, determined, and careful, he ignored the sound of the crackling gunfire aimed his way and walked toward the roadblock. As the bullets whistled past him, he

A tanker in the 761st Tank Battalion looks up from his turret

securely attached the cable to the fallen tree and then walked back to his tank. Amazingly, he was never hit. Ruben used the tank's massive power to tear the tree loose and dragged the big trunk out of the way. The roadway was opened and the **platoon** plowed ahead to achieve their objective.

Ruben's brave efforts that day won him a Silver Star, the nation's third highest award for valor. The staff sergeant's prompt action, the citation stated, "prevented a serious delay in the offensive action and was instrumental in the successful assault and capture" of Vic-sur-Seille.

Born in Tecumseh, Oklahoma, Ruben grew up in nearby Hotulka. His parents owned a farm, and along with his eleven brothers and sisters, Ruben had his hands full working the land and growing enough crops to put food on the table for fourteen hungry mouths.

When he graduated from high school, work on the railroad gave Ruben an opportunity to see some of the country. But in 1942, World War II was raging and he and two of his brothers left Oklahoma to join in the fight against the Germans and the Japanese.

After his basic training, Ruben was excited to learn

he had been assigned to a new combat unit. He traveled to Camp Hood in Texas to train with the all-black 761st Tank Battalion. This unit was nicknamed the "Black Panthers" and they trained night and day with much energy and high morale. They wanted to prove what they could do – that society was wrong about how well they could fight. But even though they always performed well in training exercises, the Army would not let them fight. They knew that white units had gone to war after only two months, but after two years, they were still waiting. Ruben was sick and tired of the waiting.

Finally, in the summer of 1944, they got their chance. Not only were the Black Panthers being put into service, they had been assigned to General George S. Patton's Third Army. Patton was known as Old Blood and Guts. He was as tough on his men as he was on the Germans, but he was one of the best generals in the Army. He told the 761st he only had the best soldiers in his army and didn't care what color they were as long as they were good soldiers. He told them they were the first black tankers to go into combat and all their people were watching them. "Don't let them down," he told them, and "don't let me down!"

THE SCOOP:
BLACK SOLDIERS IN PATTON'S ARMY

Patton's well-known racism was an attitude fostered and supported by the U.S. Army. Despite the fact that African-Americans had served with distinction extending as far back as the American Revolutionary War, assumptions ran deep about the inferiority of black soldiers as combat troops. In World War I, General John J. Pershing outlined how black troops should be treated: "We must not eat with them, must not shake hands with them, seek to talk to them, or to meet with them outside the requirements of military service."

In an effort to ensure support for the war from the African-American community, blacks were accepted into the military and allowed to train and fill much-needed support roles: loading convoy trucks, driving supply trucks and ambulances, constructing military highways, serving as cooks in the mess halls. They were kept segregated from white soldiers and were not allowed to carry a weapon. Many suffered from discrimination and cruel abuse. Still, they carried on.

"It was an ego thing," said Jehu C. Hunter, who was an officer in the 92nd Infantry. "We wanted to prove our mettle."

When it came to actual combat, black troops were kept far from the action -- until heavy casualities and a lack of replacements became an issue. It soon became obvious that, when given the chance, black soldiers were among the finest fighting men in Patton's Army.

To learn more, read *Patton's Panthers: the African-American 761st Tank Battalion in World War II*, by Charles W. Sasser.

Black tankers enter the German town of Coburg in their light tank, 1945.

Photo: National Archives

Ruben's brother soldiers remembered him as a man who chose his words carefully and who was willing to listen. Ruben was tall and lean, with features hinting at his Native American ancestry. He had a warm smile, but also a stubborn streak and a strong will. Those who knew him well admired him for his leadership skills and his fierceness in combat.

"Ruben Rivers was good, and he probably would have been an officer. No, he probably would have been company commander," said his commanding officer, Captain David J. Williams.

That opportunity, however, would not come. Hard fighting continued as the 104th Infantry fought their way toward Morville-les-Vic. While leading a group of tanks over a railroad crossing near the small village of Guebling, Ruben's vehicle hit a mine. It caused a lot of damage and sent a piece of turret into the staff sergeant's right leg, slashing it open to the bone from knee to thigh. It was an injury that should have sent him back to the field hospital, out of harm's way, and eventually back home.

Allowing the medics to clean, disinfect and bandage the wound, Ruben waved away a shot of **morphine** and turned down an offer to be driven to the aid station. He knew Captain Williams was going to need him in the battle ahead, and refused to leave the crew of his tank. Hobbling over to another tank

> **Morphine**
> A form of opium used in medicine as a painkiller

commanded by a lesser officer, he and his crew took charge of it. When medics checked on Ruben days later, the leg showed signs of infection. Again, Ruben was ordered to evacuate. He wouldn't budge.

"My Negro side says it hurts, my Indian side says it don't hurt, so I'll make it all right," he said.

On the morning of November 19th, the 761st again

pushed forward into heavy fire. Ruben had his eyes peeled for the German anti-tank guns responsible for knocking out several of his fellow tankers.

"I see them. We'll fight them," he radioed.

Ruben led the charge, but he was killed when his tank was destroyed by a direct hit from an 88mm round. His heroic act – repeatedly refusing evacuation while continuing to direct his tank's fire at enemy positions, resulting in the killing of more than 300 enemy soldiers during less than two weeks of his short combat career – moved Captain Williams to recommend Ruben for a Medal of Honor in 1944. It would take more than fifty years for his recommendation to be fulfilled.

The Black Panthers served with distinction in Europe during World War II. Because of racism in the segregated armed forces, no black soldier was given a Medal of Honor. Staff Sergeant Ruben Rivers was one of seven African-American soldiers who were eventually awarded the Medal of Honor, although this official recognition, presided over by President Bill Clinton, was not made until 1997. Captain Williams was there to make sure Ruben got his medal.

Exploration

Reading

Abdul-Jabar, Kareem, and Anthony Walton. *Brothers in Arms: the Epic Story of the 761st Tank Battalion, WWII's Forgotten Heroes.* New York: Broadway Books, 2004.

Potter, Lou. *Liberators: Fighting on Two Fronts in World War II.* New York: Harcourt, 1992.

Sasser, Charles W. *Patton's Panthers: the African-American 761st Tank Battalion in World War II.* New York : Pocket Books, 2004.

Wilson, Dale E. (Dec. 1993). "A Time to Live; a Time to Die: the Sad Saga of Staff Sergeant Ruben Rivers – African Americans and World War II." *Negro History Bulletin.*

Internet Resources

761st Tank Battalion and Allied Veterans Association
http://www.761st.com

African Americans in the U. S. Army
http://www.army.mil/africanamericans/main_content.html

Places to Visit

761st Tank Battalion Memorial
Fort Hood, Texas (near Killeen , Texas)

General George Patton Museum and the
United States Army Armor Center Memorial Park
4554 Fayette Avenue, Fort Knox, Kentucky

Learn more at our website: www.fortysixthstarpress.com/extracredit.html

9

FELICIA DAUGHERTY
Duty and Decency

The condition of the home was appalling. A musty straw-like smell hung in the air, along with the stench of unwashed bodies. A young mother, so weak she could not move from the bed, reached out in a feverish daze. In the bed with her was a tiny infant. The baby was dead. The child's mother had been too weak to even close its eyes.

Felicia Daugherty, acting as a volunteer for the American Red Cross, put a cool hand to the young woman's brow.

"I'm here," she said, her dark eyes filled with concern. "Everything is going to be fine."

It was the fall of 1918. The people of the United States had their eyes turned toward Western Europe, where American Doughboys were participating in what would later be known as the Great War, or World War I. But something new and terrible was brewing which would soon stretch every available resource: Spanish **influenza**.

> **Influenza**
>
> A highly contagious and often severe viral disease which attacks the body's respiratory system

On September 26, 1918, an Oklahoma City doctor treated a patient with symptoms very similar to what had been seen on the East coast. By Tuesday, October 1, the city was under siege as 5,000 people suddenly fell ill. Spanish influenza had arrived.

Over the next few days, the city was brought to its knees as scores of healthy, hard-working citizens of Oklahoma City came down with influenza. The mayor and other city officials were ill; hospitals were filled to capacity; and doctors and nurses were working double shifts. With the city government crippled, the American Red Cross came to the rescue. Already mobilized for the war effort, the Oklahoma City chapter used all their supplies and manpower to fight the influenza **pandemic**. Many women were already active in the Red Cross efforts, but it was Felicia who stepped up and became the leader in the fight against the deadly virus.

> **Pandemic**
>
> Occurring over a wide geographic area and affecting a high proportion of the population

According to family lore, Felicia Alberta Mitchell was born on a riverboat in Mississippi River in 1879. Such an adventurous beginning might explain her approach to life. She was a "take charge" kind of woman, never afraid to face down adversity.

She married Charles Lemuel Daugherty, from Denton, Texas, and the two eventually moved to Oklahoma City

The Spanish Influenza Pandemic

The Spanish influenza pandemic of 1918-1919 was among the most deadly in world history. Only the Black Death plague in the Middle Ages rivals Spanish influenza in terms of the number of people afflicted and the number of those killed by the disease.

This strain of the influenza A virus (later to be called H1N1) likely came from birds and proved to be highly infectious. About 20-30% of the population would get the disease and 5-10% of them would die. All this, of course, was unknown to public health officials and medical researchers. It was not even known that influenza was a virus at the time.

Scientists now believe that the flu originated in Kansas and was carried to Europe by American soldiers in March, 1918. Over the spring and summer, the flu spread across Europe. It was called the Spanish influenza because most of the early reports of the pandemic came from Spain which was not in the war and thus did not suffer from wartime restrictions on the media. By the fall it had returned to the U. S. and spread from coast to coast. About 675,000 Americans died from the deadly virus.

Although there is no cure for it, Spanish influenza vanished as quickly as it came. But not before over 50 million people had been killed around the world.

Policemen like these in Seattle in December, 1918, were on the front lines of the battle against Spanish influenza.

Photo: National Archives

where Charles pursued a career in politics. As a woman of wealth and privilege, Felicia took up the hobby of china painting, ordering blank plates from European companies, hand painting the designs, and then firing them in a kiln she had installed in the basement of her own home. Not known for her cooking skills (she'd even burn toast, her youngest son once said), Felicia relied on a large array of servants to keep her large house running smoothly. In addition to caring for her sons Philip and Frederick, she put her energy into working with the Red Cross. Her fearlessness and organizational skills would be the key to the success of Oklahoma City's fight against the influenza pandemic.

Felicia believed there were many people in the city who remained untreated. Because the transportation and communication systems were down, doctors only knew about the cases that came to them. She began recruiting women who would be willing to go into the homes of sick people and care for them. The call went out in the local newspaper:

"Every strong, competent woman who knows how to take the temperature of a patient, who can give a bath, make a bed, who can bring order to a chaotic house and who can cheer the members of a family is needed in the present crisis."

Felicia worked tirelessly: some claimed she worked 48 hours without sleeping at times. When hospitals were unable to keep up with the demand for supplies, she would call people asking for donations. She visited homes hit hard by the flu, bringing food, cleaning the home and doing the laundry. As quickly as she arrived, she'd be gone, off to help someone else. On many occasions, she'd use her own car as an ambulance to transport the worst cases to a hospital.

The Red Cross already had sewing rooms set up to make bandages and socks for the soldiers overseas. Instructions came from Red Cross headquarters to put all efforts into making flu masks and other items for influenza victims. Meanwhile, **quarantines** were ordered, schools were closed, and all other places of public gathering – churches, concert halls, theaters and bars – were temporarily shut down. Police were ordered to arrest people seen spitting in public or issue them fines.

Quarantine

The isolation of persons or goods to prevent the spread of contagious disease

Making her rounds throughout the crisis, Felicia had witnessed many tragic scenes in the city. At the home of the

Harding family, both parents had become ill with influenza. Mrs. Harding soon died and left Mr. Harding with a tiny baby and a two-year-old. He was so ill he couldn't care for the children and the baby died. Neighbors phoned the police to send for help to bury the mother and baby and find someone to care for the toddler.

Though exhausted, Felicia was undaunted. She found conditions in the city, especially among the poor and working classes, to be deplorable and she was very frustrated by the lack of care, concern and heart displayed by city leaders, both at city hall and in the medical profession. After filling

A New York City mailman protects himself against the deadly Spanish influenza virus, October, 1918.

the hallways and closets with beds and pulling every medical student out of class to administer care, the hospitals had stopped taking new patients, especially those who could not pay. For some reason, though, authorities refused to open the city's Detention Hospital, which had recently closed due to staff shortages. There were also stories of the sick not getting medicine because they could not pay for it. These problems infuriated Felicia, and she appealed to city leaders to do something about the problems.

At first they refused, but eventually the Detention Hospital was opened, making 100 new beds available. It wasn't enough. Felicia complained to the city commissioner and he quickly arranged for the city to commandeer rooming houses downtown to house patients at the city's expense. The city also agreed to foot the bill for each influenza patient admitted to a local hospital.

Felicia continued to plead with anyone who would listen to her description of how perilous conditions were in the city. Her example made some less dedicated officials appear to be shirking their duties. One official, Mark Kesler, accused her of playing politics in the hopes of having him fired.

THE SCOOP:
STRONG, HEALTHY, YOUNG — AND SICK

Spanish influenza differed from earlier flu epidemics in its severity. Within hours of being stricken, victims were incapacitated, unable to walk or even move their arms and legs in some cases. A fever of 100 to 104 degrees lasting three to four days was common, as was a heavy cough. The skin would turn blue and sometimes black, so much so that sometimes a patient's race could not be determined. In severe cases, blood would fill the lungs and the stricken person would drown in their own body fluids.

"After gasping for several hours they became delirious and incontinent, and many died struggling to clear their airways of a blood-tinged froth that sometimes gushed from their nose and mouth. It was a dreadful business," wrote a medical student from the University of Pennsylvania.

Another strange characteristic of Spanish influenza soon became apparent. This new strain seemed to attack strong, healthy young and middle-aged people. Just as it struck hard at the virile young soldiers in Europe and U.S. Army bases, it seemed to target the healthy hard-working citizens of the country.

Children had their own ways of coping, even coming up with a jump rope song that spread through playgrounds around the country:

I had a little bird
And its name was Enza
I opened the window
And in-flew-Enza.

In response to Kesler's attacks against her character, a special commission meeting was called. Felicia was asked to tell her side of the affair. She gave a passionate defense and closed by saying, "The business of combating this epidemic, in plain English, means that sick people shall not be left to die simply because they are poor. Mr. Kesler can call it "politics" if he wants to, but those of us who are not politicians regard it as simple Christian duty and humanitarian decency." After Felicia's plea, Kesler resigned and control of all city health facilities was given to the Red Cross.

As usual, Felicia and the Red Cross were prepared. A three-part plan of action was drawn up. First, the worst cases were identified and admitted to a hospital. Second, milder cases and those recovering were provided with better food, clean clothes and had their homes disinfected. Third, to help prevent relapse, volunteers were called to literally scrub down the city: streets paved with brick would be hosed down and washed with soap, dirt streets would be raked, and **vermin** chased out of dark corners and sent packing.

Vermin

Small harmful animals that are difficult to control

INFLUENZA

Spread by Droplets sprayed from Nose and Throat

Cover each COUGH and SNEEZE with handkerchief.

Spread by contact.

AVOID CROWDS.

If possible, WALK TO WORK.

Do not spit on floor or sidewalk.

Do not use common drinking cups and common towels.

Avoid excessive fatigue.

If taken ill, go to bed and send for a doctor.

The above applies also to colds, bronchitis, pneumonia, and tuberculosis.

Felicia arranged for additional temporary hospital wards to be set up. Groceries were purchased at city expense and police were ordered to assist in the delivery of meals. Many civic clubs whose members owned cars also volunteered.

The tide in the battle against Spanish influenza turned almost overnight. Once the Red Cross began removing infected people from homes and getting them early care, the number of new cases dropped dramatically. Doctors, nurses, and the early volunteers could now get some rest after two weeks of round-the-clock shifts.

On November 9, the ban on public gathering was lifted. It was a Saturday night and the whole city rejoiced. Theaters and dance halls were packed. Spirits were raised by news that Germany had surrendered – the Great War had ended. On Sunday, the people came together to worship when churches opened for the first time in over a month. The people of Oklahoma City had weathered one of the most trying times in the city's short history. With the help of Felicia Daugherty, they had battled hand-to-hand with war, death, and disease, and emerged victorious.

Exploration

Reading

Aron, Virginia. *The Influenza Pandemic of 1918*. Philadelphia, Penn.: Chelsea House, 2000.

Getz, David. *Purple Death: the Mysterious Flu of 1918*. New York: Henry Holt and Co., 2000.

Peters, Stephanie True. *The 1918 Influenza Pandemic*. New York: Benchmark Books, 2005.

Internet Resources

American Experience: Influenza 1918
http://www.pbs.org/wgbh/amex/influenza/
an exploration of the pandemic through American eyes

Centers for Disease Control and Prevention: Pandemic Flu
http://www.pandemicflu.gov/index.html
find out about the ongoing fight against pandemic flu

National Archives and Records Administration
The Deadly Virus: The Influenza Epidemic of 1918
http://www.archives.gov/exhibits/influenza-epidemic/

Secrets of the Dead: Killer Flu
http://www.pbs.org/wnet/secrets/case_killerflu/index.html
medical researchers track down the deadly Spanish flu virus

Places to Visit

National Museum of Health and Medicine
Walter Reed Army Hospital
6900 Georgia Avenue NW, Washington, D. C.

Learn more at our website: www.fortysixthstarpress.com/extracredit.html

ROBBIE RISNER
Resist to the Utmost

"Yea, though I walk through the valley of the shadow of death, I will fear no evil."

Colonel Robinson "Robbie" Risner kept his eyes on the back of the room. More guards were gathering, their eyes burning with fury as the men continued saying the beloved Psalm in unison.

> **Fact File**
> James Robinson Risner
> "Robbie"
> Born: January 16, 1925
> Mammoth Spring, Ark.
> Grew up in: Tulsa, Okla.

To the American prisoners of war (POW) gathered in Room 7 of the Hoa Lo prison, it was a simple church service. To the prison guards, used to Communist political indoctrination sessions, it was a POW-led call to rebellion. Groups of withered men, worn down by brutal torture sessions, lack of food, no access to proper medical care, and denied their rights and privileges under the **Geneva Conventions**, gathered to sing familiar hymns, quote the Twenty-third Psalm, and recite the Pledge of Allegiance together.

> **Geneva Conventions**
>
> A series of agreements made in Geneva, Switzerland, which established rules for the treatment of prisoners of war

"For thou art with me. Thy rod and thy staff, they comfort me."

Despite multiple orders from their North Vietnamese captors to stop, the men continued. Each saw this small act of rebellion as a symbolic gesture, something to hold onto in the hopes that their release was approaching. It was February 7th, 1971, a day that would later come to be known as "The Church Riot."

War in Vietnam

Shortly after World War II ended in 1945, the United States entered into a competition for influence with the Soviet Union. This was known as the Cold War because instead of directly fighting each other the two powers took sides in wars in other countries. The U. S. believed in the Domino Theory – if one free country fell to Communism, then all the others around it would, too. They decided that Communism had to be contained in the countries where it had spread. Therefore, the U. S. was willing to fight wars overseas to make sure Communism was held in check.

One of these wars took place in the southeast Asian nation of Vietnam. This small country had been a colony of France, but France was weakened after World War II and could not maintain her control over Vietnam. A war of independence began. France was defeated by the rebels in 1954 and Vietnam was split in two – North Vietnam was Communist and South Vietnam modeled itself after the American system.

North Vietnam wanted to unify the country as a single Communist nation and began working with the Viet Cong, a Communist group in the South with the same goal. The U. S. feared the South would fall to the Communists, so in 1956 it began sending military advisors to train the South's army. The U. S. gradually sent more advisors to South Vietnam until 1965, when larger numbers of troops began to arrive. By 1969, there were over 500,000 American troops in Vietnam. Meanwhile, the Soviet Union and China provided supplies and guidance to the North Vietnamese.

Back home, many Americans were unhappy with the war; massive anti-war protests were staged in the major cities, while some who originally supported the war grew weary of it as years passed with no peaceful resolution. By 1973, the United States could no longer bear the economic or human costs of the war and entered into a peace agreement with the North. The U. S. agreed to withdraw its troops if the North agreed not to attack the South. However, with American troops gone and the American government crippled by the Watergate scandal, the North did attack and overrun the South in April, 1975. The long war had ended.

During the U. S. involvement in Vietnam (1961-1975), over 58,000 Americans died, over 300,000 were wounded and nearly 2,000 are still missing.

"Surely goodness and mercy will follow me all the days of my life, and I will dwell in the house of the Lord forever."

As the senior ranking officer (SRO) in the Hanoi Hilton (as the Americans mockingly called Hoa Lo prison), Robbie had organized the common church service. Moving forward to give a prayer, he eyeballed the guards who were becoming increasingly nervous. Bayonets fixed and ready, they came forward and took Robbie away for **interrogation** and torture.

> **Interrogation**
>
> To examine or gather information from someone by asking a series of questions

At first, no one moved. Then, to lend support to the SRO, a man they loved and admired for his leadership during the pain and hardship of POW life, the men burst into "The Star-Spangled Banner," a song none had dared to sing in their many years in prison.

The men sang at the top of their lungs. When Robbie heard them, he straightened his back and held his head high. "I felt like I was nine feet tall and could go bear hunting with a switch," he said later.

He was born in Mammoth Spring, Arkansas, but Robbie grew up in Eastern Oklahoma. The family first moved

116

HANOI HILTON

The notorious Hoa Lo Prison was built by the French in 1904.
The American POWs gave it the ironic nickname Hanoi Hilton.

to Pumpkin Center, Oklahoma, living on oil-lease land while his father traded cattle and horses. In the evening, the smell of oil and gas and the sound of the oil well pumps would lull Robbie and his brothers and his sisters to sleep.

The family moved on to Sapulpa, and then to Tulsa. There, Robbie became involved with the youth at the First Assembly of God Church. He worked as a stock clerk for the Chamber of Commerce, took an occasional job welding, and maintained the cars on his father's used car lot.

After graduating from Central High School in Tulsa, Robbie pursued a dream that he'd had for a long time: becoming a pilot. When he turned eighteen, he was eager to join the Air Force. One requirement was to provide an official birth certificate. Robbie found the country doctor had left off part of his name. Instead of James Robinson Risner, the certificate read "Robinson Risner." Even though he'd been called James, Jamey or Jim for 18 years, he decided to go by "Robbie" from that moment.

Before long, Robbie became one of the most accomplished fighter pilots in the history of the United States Air Force. He met and married a nurse named Kathleen Shaw, and went on to earn the elite title of ace, which meant he had shot down five enemy aircraft in combat. Decorated for service in the Korean War due to dramatic success in **dog fights**, he was shot down twice during his service in Vietnam. The first time was in April, 1965. He was rescued and returned to duty, and even made the cover of *Time* magazine. In September, 1965 his luck ran

Dog fight
Combat between two or more fighter planes

Four F-105 fighters and a B-66 bomber on a bombing run over North Vietnam in 1966.

out: his F-105 Thunderchief jet was shot down and Robbie was captured by the North Vietnamese, beginning his seven-year experience as a POW.

At first, Robbie's captors were rather lenient. They wanted him to admit his "criminal behavior" and apologize for his actions against the Vietnamese people. Robbie knew that prisoners of war were accorded certain rights and recognitions under the Geneva Conventions, and he refused to be intimidated.

He was thrown into a concrete room adjoining cells where other American soldiers were being held. They spent some time going over camp rules that would keep the new POW out of trouble and taught him a code using taps on the concrete that would help him communicate with other prisoners. Later, Robbie ordered all prisoners in the Hanoi Hilton to secretly communicate by the tap code without the knowledge of the North Vietnamese. In terms of morale, it was one of the most important orders issued to the Americans, giving them purpose and direction in resisting their captors.

When he was caught giving orders, policies or suggestions to the other airmen, Robbie was tortured. All that he knew about torture had been learned from books and magazines. He believed he would be able to withstand the pain and would never reveal anything. But the reality of torture was very different than what he'd seen at the movies. The hours of **excruciating** punishment on his body began to take a toll. Even worse was the psychological torture. After days of

> **Excruciating**
> Causing great pain or anguish

inhuman treatment, he eventually agreed to write a confession

THE SCOOP:
INSIDE THE MIND OF AN AIR CREW

Lieutenant Tom Herskowitz was a RIO, Radar Intercept Officer, in the backseat of a U. S. Navy F-4 Phantom jet. His squadron, The Freelancers (VF-21), operated off the aircraft carrier U.S.S. *Ranger* in 1970-71. They flew hundreds of missions deep into enemy territory to stop the flow of troops and supplies entering South Vietnam through Laos.

"I did not know any of the POWs first hand, but they influenced all our flights. Just the thought of being a POW did affect what we would do. My pilot, Jack Hayes, and I had decided that if we ever got in a dog fight we would press the attack even if it meant losing our plane. But, we would not do that if it meant we would have to eject over land controlled by the enemy. There was no risk worth taking if it meant time in the Hanoi Hilton.

I was in Vietnam after Doug Hegdahl had been released and we knew what was happening to our men in Hanoi. We knew there was a risk of getting killed, wounded, shot down, or captured, or some combination thereof. There was also a feeling that we did control some of our destiny. The way you rolled in on a target; what you would do if you were hit; how you could nurse a sick plane back over the beach and get "feet wet" so that you could be picked up by friendlies. This gave us confidence. But we knew that our fellow aviators were just as good or better than us and they got bagged. So the awareness was always there, even if pushed to the back of our minds."

dictated by his torturers.

"To make it, I prayed by the hour," Robbie wrote in his autobiography, *The Passing of the Night*. "It was automatic, almost subconscious. I did not ask God to take me out of it. I prayed he would give me strength to endure it. When it got so bad that I did not think I could stand it, I would ask God to ease it and somehow I would make it." Faith in God, and the images of his wife and five sons back home, helped Robbie focus through the pain.

Off and on during his time as a POW, Robbie spent more than three years in solitary confinement. Nevertheless, he continued to lead the American resistance in the North Vietnamese prison complex, endearing himself to the men with his faith and optimism. He urged them to "resist to the utmost, give as little as possible, and then recover to resist again."

Four essential beliefs gave Robbie and the other POWs the strength to hang on during the difficult times: a belief that they were fighting Communism, which was an enemy of freedom; that they were fulfilling a duty to their country; that the American people were behind them; and finally, that God would bring them all out of prison as better men.

After Robbie was released in February of 1973, he traveled to Oklahoma City where he was given a welcome home parade by the people of Warr Acres, the suburb in which he and his family lived. "The future was before me. The doors that were locked and closed were now unlocked and permanently open. The darkness of that long, unbelievable night had finally passed," he wrote in the ending lines of his autobiography.

Among his many awards, Robbie is a double recipient of the Air Force Cross the second highest military decoration that can be awarded to a member of the United States Air Force. In 1974, he was initiated into the Oklahoma Hall of Fame. He retired as a Brigadier General in 1976.

"I would go to the ends of the earth to follow this man," said Lt. Cmdr. Everett Alvarez, the first American pilot to be captured and held captive for eight and a half years. "Robbie Risner ... was a great leader and a very brave man."

Exploration

Reading

Alvarez, Everett and Anthony S. Pitch. *Chained Eagle.* New York : Donald I. Fine, 1989.

Risner, Robinson. *The Passing of the Night: My Seven Years as a Prisoner of the North Vietnamese.* New York : Random House, 1973.

Rochester , Stuart I. and Frederick Kiley. *Honor Bound: American Prisoners of War in Southeast Asia, 1961-1973.* Annapolis , Md. Naval Institute Press, 1999.

Internet Resources

American Experience: Return with Honor
http://www.pbs.org/wgbh/amex/honor/index.html
a moving story of American prisoners of war in Vietnam

American Experience: Vietnam Online
http://www.pbs.org/wgbh/amex/vietnam/index.html
online companion to Vietnam: a Television History

Experiencing War: Prisoners of War
http://www.loc.gov/vets/stories/pow-korea.html
stories from the Veteran's History Project

Places to Visit

Brigadier General Robinson Risner Statue
Air Garden, United States Air Force Academy
Colorado Springs, Colo.

Vietnam Veterans Memorial
National Mall, Washington, D. C.

Learn more at our website: www.fortysixthstarpress.com/extracredit.html

Index

S

T

V

W

About the Creators

Jana Hausburg is a cataloger for the Metropolitan Library System of Oklahoma City. Always fascinated by stories, she first picked up a pen and started writing at the age of 3 1/2. Unfortunately she could not yet spell, so the manuscript remains unpublished. The three historical figures she would like to challenge in a game of Scrabble are Dorothy Parker, Robert Benchley, and Mark Twain. She resides in Bethany, Oklahoma with her husband and two sons.

Cheryl Delany is a graduate of Southern Nazarene University and obtained her MBA in Advertising Art from San Antonio College. As a child, she often got in trouble for daydreaming and sketching in class because drawing pirate treasure, mummies and ghosts was a lot more fun than listening to the teacher! Now she works out of a studio nestled in the mountains outside of Denver, Colorado, where she lives with her husband.

FSC